TOILET
LEARNING

Also by Alison Mack

DRY ALL NIGHT: The Picture Book Technique That Stops Bedwetting

This book
is a gift from
The Teacher Center
In memory of
Corinne Levin

TOILET LEARNING

The Picture Book Technique for Children and Parents

by Alison Mack

Pictures by George C. Phillips

Foreword by Paul L. Adams, M.D.

LITTLE, BROWN AND COMPANY
Boston — New York — London

Toilet Learning, The Picture Book Technique, and *The Picture
Book Technique for Children and Parents* are trademarks of
Alison Mack.

LIBRARY OF CONGRESS CATALOGING IN PUBLICATION DATA
Mack, Alison.
    Toilet learning.

    1. Toilet training.   I. Title.
HQ770.5.M3   649'.6   77-24305
ISBN 0-316-54233-4 (hc)
ISBN 0-316-54237-7 (pb)

17 16 15 14

MV

Foreword

Most books on child rearing take the viewpoint that coexistence or détente between parent and child is very arduous to maintain. These books become, therefore, manuals on how to outsmart and trick children, or, more euphemistically, to bring the child's behavior under parental control without the child's knowing what hit him. Alison Mack's book does none of this. Instead, it is open, direct, and respectful of the child's real needs and wishes.

The basic ideas permeating this book are that we were made to live with children, that parenting is a happy time of giving, that we benefit from the parent-to-child relationship even if it is a demanding one, and that children will do a good enough job of enculturation if we let them go at their own speed. To let children take an interest in their own independence and autonomy — and take hold of their toileting when they are good and ready to do so — is a sound and modest proposal.

One would wish that all kinds of parents will have easy access to this book; working mothers, single parents, and parents with little formal schooling should benefit from it. When the child is foremost, as in *Toilet Learning* the child is, a universality emerges.

The early preschool years are a time of much learning and joy if one serves the child in a spirit of empathic helpfulness. Alison Mack describes what fun that can be for both adult and child. If parents have good sense, they will not stress toilet training. But parents will help their child in the best way possible — as described in this book — to add toilet *learning* to the overall vast learning and widening of vistas that take place in this delightful period. Mack's book is sound psychiatry, sound pedagogy, morally sound and humanistic. I foresee a good future for *Toilet Learning* not only among children and parents, but among early childhood educators, pediatricians, and parent counselors as well.

Paul L. Adams, M.D.
Department of Psychiatry and Behavioral Sciences
School of Medicine
University of Louisville
Louisville, Kentucky

Acknowledgments

I am grateful to Ron Blackman for his invaluable contribution to this book. I benefited greatly from the advice and assistance of Frank Caplan, Director of the Princeton Center for Infancy & Early Childhood; Lester Coleman, M.D.; Dr. Graciela Coons; Dr. Richard Gelles, of the University of Rhode Island Department of Sociology; Morrison Levbarg, M.D.; Hedy Lipez, R.N.; Peter Moss, Research Officer of the University of London Institute of Education; Ernest Pilz, M.D., of Glanzing Kinderklinik, Vienna; Mrs. Norman Rockwell; Barton Schmitt, M.D., Director of the Child Protection Team at Colorado General Hospital; Dr. and Mrs. Arthur Wasser, M.D.; Gilbert Wise, M.D., Director of Urology, Maimonides Medical Center; Professor Marcella Mazarelli, of the Williams College Department of Anthropology; Professors Arlene Amidon and Phebe Cramer, Ph.D., of the Williams Department of Psychology; and the teachers of the WIZO Day Care Nurseries, Tel Aviv.

Dr. Martha Bernal of the University of Denver Department of Psychology; Dr. John Bowlby; Dr. Preston Bruce, of the

Office of Child Development, U.S. Department of Health, Education and Welfare; Donald Cohen, M.D., of the Yale University Child Study Center; Dr. Anna Freud, Director of the Hampstead Child-Therapy Course and Clinic, London; Professor M. L. Hoffman, of the University of Michigan Department of Psychology; Dr. Frances Horowitz, of the University of Kansas Department of Human Development; Ruth Kempe, M.D., of the National Center for the Prevention and Treatment of Child Abuse and Neglect; Professor Rolf Peterson of the University of Illinois Department of Psychology; Naomi Richman, M.D., of the Hospital for Sick Children, London; Dr. James Robertson; the American Academy of Pediatrics; the National Institute of Child Health and Human Development; Section on Clinical Child Psychology of the American Psychological Association; Sigmund Freud Society, Vienna; and the University of Illinois Institute for Child Behavior and Development supplied valuable information.

Special thanks go to Mary Goodwin, M.D., who gave me the benefit of more than forty years of pediatric practice in making many wise suggestions. Finally, I wish to express my appreciation to the children and parents who participated in the development and testing of this book.

Alison Mack

Contents

This book is for Max

1

Parents' Guide to Toilet Learning

Bowel and bladder training has become the most obviously disturbing item of child training in wide circles of our society.
　　　　　　　　—Erik Erikson, *Childhood and Society*

Toilet Learning

When the people of the Indonesian island of Alor were asked by an anthropologist when a child is ready to learn bowel and bladder control, their answer was simple: "When the child is old enough to understand."

The most important decision you will be called upon to make during your child's early years may be when to begin teaching him to use the toilet. If you start too soon or too late, it will be harder for you and your child. This book presents a technique which will help you help your child learn bladder and bowel control. By judging the extent to which your child understands the book's pictures and text and expresses interest in the subject, you will be able to tell when he is ready to learn to take charge of his bodily functions. When he is ready, it will help you teach him.

Part 1 of this book is for you. It clears up the confusion which surrounds this single greatest problem area of early childhood, and gives you the knowledge you will need to get your child

3

out of diapers without wrecking your nerves or his. It includes a page-by-page guide to Part 2, beginning on page 33.

Part 2 is for your child. As you read the text aloud, each step in the process of toilet learning is explained in language that will be understood by a child who is ready, while the illustrations demonstrate the behavior that's expected. By watching your child's reactions to the words and pictures, and by asking questions to see how much he understands, you will be able to tell when to introduce him to the mysteries of the bathroom and his own body. As he makes progress he can look at Part 2 again and again by himself. Unlike toilet training, which was something grown-ups did to a child, toilet learning is something a child does himself.

If you thought that a child who was about to be toilet trained would be too young to understand a book, you were right. Old-fashioned toilet training, as compared with the program of toilet learning which this book sets forth, was often begun during the first year. Toilet training was just that: a form of training, such as one would use to housebreak a puppy. Its goal, in a day when getting diapers clean meant endless drudgery, was to ease the burden on overworked mothers. No attention was paid to whether the child was physically and psychologically ready. Today, washing machines, diaper services, and disposable diapers have lessened the tendency to train kids before age 2, when they begin to be able to have real control.

In order for the child to control the bowels and bladder voluntarily, the nervous and excretory systems must reach a level of development that may come by age 2, age 3, or later. If you begin teaching your child before he's ready, he'll want to cooperate but lack the coordination necessary to do so. If you begin long after your child becomes ready, the effort and expense of diapers will continue that much longer, and you may miss the period of peak readiness during which the child will learn most easily.

Fortunately, nature is pretty clever. The muscular control and the understanding needed for toilet learning arrive at about the same time. The maturity of your child's insides is, of course, hard to measure. But comprehension and interest in the principles involved can be observed. The purpose of Part 2 is to make it possible for you to observe them. When you see that your child understands what is going on in Part 2, you will know that he's ready to begin learning how to use the toilet.

This book has undergone extensive pre-publication field-testing with children from many backgrounds. The children followed their parents' presentation of Part 2 with rapt attention. When the last page had been turned, many kids wanted to go right back to the beginning and start all over again. Several mothers and fathers told me it was the longest time their youngsters had ever sat still. Part 2 of this book attracts a child's interest by showing real people doing real things — things that he can do too. Children at this stage think of books as a source of enjoyment. Seeing the steps in toilet learning illustrated in a book of their own will lead them to think of the whole process as being enjoyable. Your child will be eager to rise to the occasion of being asked to study a book along with his parents. He'll want to move quickly from "book learning" to actually using the bathroom. At the same time, the child's interest in reading will be increased, because this book is about his favorite subject: himself.

One last word before you use this book: *Relax*. Many mothers and fathers are concerned that teaching their children bowel and bladder control is a mysteriously powerful parent-child interaction fraught with all sorts of hidden pitfalls, any one of which can induce crippling neurosis. But in reality, toilet learning is no different from any other early childhood learning experience — learning how to handle a fork, or button a shirt — that requires a combination of mental and muscular coordination. Unless a parent's anxiety makes it "special," toilet learning will be viewed by most children as just another learning experience. The purpose of this book is to reinforce the naturalness of this learning process. By seeing the steps in toilet learning shown in pictures just like those in his other books, the child will see that going to the bathroom is simply another normal human activity.

Yet looked at another way, toilet learning is uniquely important. It will be the first time you teach your child a complex behavior pattern. The way you do it will be a touchstone of your entire relationship with your child. Toilet learning presents a remarkable opportunity to evaluate your entire approach to child rearing as your personality and your child's become revealed to you.

The Toilet Trained Mother

Infant Care is the bestselling United States government publication of all time. It is fascinating to look through its early editions, which offered what was thought to be the best child-rearing advice available at the time, much of which seems very strange today. For example, the first *Infant Care*, issued in 1914, insisted that parents not play with their baby at any time:

> The rule that parents should not play with the baby may seem hard, but it is without doubt a safe one. . . . It is a regrettable fact that the few minutes of play that the father has when he gets home at night, which is often the only time he has with the child, may result in nervous disturbance of the baby and upset his regular habits.

Among the "regular habits" which were thought to be more important than warmth between parent and child were those of elimination.

> In order to do away with the need for diapers as early in life as possible, the baby should be taught to use the chamber.

This training may be begun by the third month, or even earlier in some cases. . . . In order to be effective, the chamber must be presented to the baby at the same hour every day, usually just before the morning bath, and it must be presented persistently until the habit is formed. Much time and patience will be required on the part of the mother, but in the end the habit thus formed will be a great saving of trouble to her and of untold value to the child, not only in babyhood, but throughout the whole of life.

Incredibly, the 1921 *Infant Care* recommended that bowel training begin as soon as the baby was born. The more lenient 1929 edition suggested holding off until the ripe old age of 1 month:

The mother should hold him over the chamber, using a soap stick, if necessary, to start the movement, and continue this day after day, not varying the time by five minutes, until the baby is fixed in this habit.

Figure 1 shows the drawing that illustrated this text, which recommended that the American mother spend a great deal of time holding a "porcelain cuspidor" to her infant's rear end.

As soon as the baby was old enough to sit, it graduated to a potty chair. Children were forced to sit there for hours every day, held in by straps. "Care is . . . necessary," warned the University of Minnesota's 1930 *Child Care and Training*, "to avoid prolapse of the rectum, which sometimes occurs when the child sits too long. . . ."

Mothers were told by *Infant Care* that when the baby was 10 months old, they should begin training the bladder by presenting the pot once an hour.

Daytime control of the bladder should have been learned by most babies by 18 months of age. By this time also the baby may have learned to indicate his need.

When it spoke of control of the bowels and bladder, *Infant Care* didn't mean what we think of today as control. Certainly

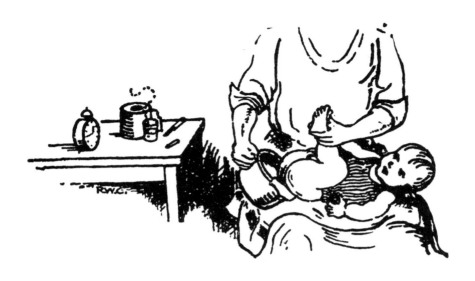

FIGURE 1

Illustration from the 1929 edition of the U.S. government's *Infant Care*: "Hold the baby in your lap or lay him on a table with his head toward your left, in the position for changing his diaper. Lift the feet with the left hand and with the right insert a soap stick or other suppository into the rectum. Still holding the feet up, press a small chamber gently against the buttocks with the right hand and hold it there until the stool is passed."

a child that was said to have "daytime control" at 18 months but could not yet "indicate his need" was not able to get to the bathroom under his own power, remove his clothing, climb up on the toilet, climb off, pull his pants up and flush. This sort of pseudo-control simply shifted the mother's time and energy from washing diapers to storming around the house trying to get the jump on her child's bodily functions. The University of Minnesota Institute of Child Welfare instructed:

> Beginning not later than one year of age, watch the child for several days and note the time it urinates. Place the child on

a vessel near the time you have noted and keep a record of the number of times you are successful in anticipating his needs. This routine procedure should take place before and after naps, immediately after meals, before going to bed, either once during the night or just before the parents retire, and directly upon arising.

What the experts of yesteryear were recommending was, in reality, not that the mother toilet train her child, but that by learning to catch her child's excreta in a porcelain cuspidor, she toilet train herself.

The Benefits of the Toilet

Why did generations of women spend their time in this odd way? Only in recent Western culture has there been an attempt to condition toilet habits before children could walk and understand simple speech. What was all the fuss about?

The biggest single factor was the desire to get out from under a pile of dirty diapers. The 1914 *Infant Care* recommended that a newborn's layette include four- to six-dozen diapers. In an era of large families, little hot water, and no washing machines, getting diapers clean was a horrendous chore. Mothers had to spend hours each day changing, scraping, scrubbing, boiling, wringing, hanging, and folding diapers. In those days, it seldom occurred to fathers that dealing with dirty diapers might be their responsibility too. The burden fell entirely on mothers. No wonder they were willing to go to any lengths to get their kids to do it in the pot.

There were other reasons, too. Doctors believed that bulky diapers caused thigh deformities. In the nineteenth century it had been thought that if a child didn't empty his bowels regularly, poisonous matter would remain in the lower intestines and be reabsorbed, with dire results. This was nonsense, of course, but the idea lasted long into the twentieth century. Women compared their mothering ability with that of other women on the basis of whose child was trained earlier. But the most important reason for early elimination training — besides the desire to "eliminate" diapers — was the belief that it was a powerful habit-building device. This idea had its roots in the nineteenth-century belief that only toilet training which took place in earliest infancy would establish "habits of cleanliness and delicacy." William P. Dewees, M.D., the Dr. Spock of the 1820s, pointed with approval to a mother who trained her infant at 1 month, and urged other mothers to try for this ideal.

In the twentieth century this notion was broadened to apply beyond the area of hygiene. John B. Watson, the psychologist whose behaviorist theories formed the basis of the recommendations in the early editions of *Infant Care*, saw toilet training as the arena in which the first struggle for parental control over the child took place. Its purpose, according to Watson's *Psychological Care of Infant and Child*, was not simply to establish habits but, more important, to teach the child to subordinate his desires to those of adults. In the 1930s toilet training was looked upon not mainly as a way of keeping a baby dry and comfortable, but as a way of giving the child a sense of order. It was not an end in itself, but merely a means to an end. This idea reached its height in Dr. Rudolf Dreikurs's 1948 *The Challenge of Parenthood*:

> The sense of order grows out of punctuality and system. [The baby] will learn the benefits of the toilet if he is put there at regular periods whether he needs to relieve himself or not.

There was, however, one major problem with beginning toilet training early: it didn't work. Mothers may have successfully trained themselves to catch their babies' movements. They may even have trained their babies to go at the same time each day. But an early beginning to training did not necessarily result in an early end. A landmark experiment to see whether starting early speeded up training was conducted in 1940 with a pair of identical twins. One twin was given early bladder training, beginning at 41 days. The other twin's training began much later, on his second birthday. Both twins achieved urinary control at the same age — 26 months. A 1957 survey reached the same conclusion: the age of beginning bowel and bladder control made no difference in the age at which control was attained. A 1962 study showed that there was a relationship between the age at which training was begun and the age at which it was finished: it found that two-thirds of the children who were still not trained by 4 years had begun training before 18 months. An early beginning to training could mean a later end.

If lack of effectiveness were the only problem with early toilet training, it wouldn't be objectionable — just not advisable. But there are other arguments against early training which are even more convincing. Though child-rearing authorities used to be unanimous in recommending early bowel training, it has since been proven that most babies' movements are not regular enough for the mother to catch. Generations of mothers were programmed to fail. Mothers didn't know this, however, so they blamed this unavoidable failure on themselves and, what was worse, projected it onto their children. Mothers who began their training attempts before a child could walk or talk were likely to interpret the child's physical inability to perform on command as stubbornness and rebellion. This led them to resort to harsh techniques. Browbeating and ridicule were common. Many mothers smacked their children if they went in their diapers or couldn't go when put on the potty. When a child messed his diaper they refused to change it "to teach him a lesson." Some mothers would threaten to smear their children's faces with excrement if they didn't shape up. There are cases reported in which children were made to eat feces as a punishment for being unable to control their bowels.

For the first time in his young life, the child was brought into conflict with society's demands and found wanting. His first experience of trying to learn a complex task was met by constant frustration at best, harsh punishment at worst. Even "successful" training often broke down during the child's third year. The child had not learned control. It had merely been trained into him. This training might work in infancy, but would not be taken into later childhood because it was not voluntary. As the child began to use language and reason after 2, the involuntary mechanism had to break down in order to be replaced by the true voluntary control that would carry into adulthood. The breakdown of control resulted in "accidents" which often gave rise to another round of punishment for apparent rebelliousness. It is interesting to speculate as to how much of the fabled terribleness of the "terrible twos" has to do with mishandled toilet training.

Early, rigid toilet training often was followed by chronic constipation and bed-wetting. These conditions brought more parental anger down on the child, which could lead to emotional disturbance. Harsh early training has been linked with aggressive behavior in children. And because the organs of elimination are near the sex organs, anxieties stirred up by rigid toilet training could easily transfer to the sexual area.

Strict toilet training is still all too common. Toilet training is, in fact, one of the most common causes of the battered child syndrome among toddlers. Dr. Barton Schmitt, Director of the Child Protection Team at Denver's Colorado General Hospital, gave me a grim rundown of toilet training–related child abuse: "Over the years we have seen a good many younger children physically abused because of resistance to toilet training or due to toilet training accidents. We have seen grab-mark bruises on the shoulders when the child was forcibly held on the potty seat. Strap marks have been observed when parents have tied the child to the potty so tightly that blood vessels under the skin ruptured. We have seen pinch-mark bruises about the genitals resulting from punishment for accidents."

The most striking injury inflicted in retaliation for toileting mishaps is the "dunking burn." This is produced when the parent holds the child's thighs against its abdomen in a jackknife position and dunks the buttocks and genital area into a bucket or tub of scalding water. This results in a circular burn restricted to the buttocks. With deeper forced immersion the scald extends higher, and down the back of the thighs. Burns account for some 10 percent of total child abuse, and the dunking burn is seen in 45 percent of these cases.

The Age of Understanding

The reason I've explored the question of early toilet training in such depth is that the most serious mistake you could make would be to start the process of toilet learning before your child is ready. One of the most important decisions you may be called on to make during your child's preschool years will be when to begin your program of toilet learning. Part 1 of this book is designed to give you the background you will need to make this decision. Part 2 will make it easy for you to judge your child's degree of readiness and act on it.

Your child's ripeness for toilet learning depends on his level of muscular, neurological, and psychological development.

The infant's excretory functions are governed at first by an automatic mechanism. When the bowels and bladder are empty or partially filled, their outlets are closed by ring-shaped muscles called sphincters. The anal and urinary sphincters are automatically kept in contraction by the sympathetic nervous system, which is not subject to conscious control. When the contents reach a certain level, the sphincters relax. At the same time, the smooth muscles of the bowels, the bladder, or both contract, pushing out the contents. As the infant's nervous system develops, this automatic mechanism is gradually replaced by a voluntary one.

In order for nerve fibers to transmit conscious impulses from the brain, they must be surrounded by a sheath composed of a fatty substance known as myelin. The process by which this sheath is formed is known as myelination. Myelination of nerves involved in bowel control takes place between the twelfth and twentieth months. So it's pointless to try to begin toilet learning before the twenty-first month. The late child development researcher Dr. Arnold Gesell put it this way: "Sphincter control . . . therefore depends not upon 'will power' but upon nerve cell structures which have to grow. All toilet training must defer to the maturity of the child's central nervous system."

As the child becomes physically ready, he also becomes psychologically ready. He becomes interested in your toilet habits. He begins to want to be in charge of his bodily functions, to be less dependent on you for his cleanliness and comfort. He becomes capable of what the Swiss developmental psychologist Jean Piaget called "deferred imitation" — the ability to watch you do something and later, without you present, do the same thing. It's impossible, of course, for a parent to determine whether a child's nerves are myelinated or to measure the capacity of a child's bladder. But the time of psychological readiness is something a sensitive parent can judge. If I could suggest only one way to tell when your child is ready, it would be the guideline used by the people of Alor:

When the child is old enough to understand: understand what you want him to do, understand why it should be done, and understand how to do it.

The two essential purposes of Part 2 of this book are

— to allow you to judge your child's degree of psychological readiness and

— to present the facts of toilet learning to your child in such a way that he'll understand fully what is expected of him.

Most likely, you will find that your child reaches peak readiness for toilet learning around 2½. At about this age children often spontaneously develop a desire to do things on their own which increases their interest in controlling their bodies. Some kids feel this need so strongly that they begin to insist on doing absolutely everything without help from their parents — dressing and undressing, bathing, getting in and out of the car. Since diapering requires a great deal of adult assistance, there could be no better time to introduce the child to toilet learning than during this stage. The child will enjoy being taught how to use the bathroom because he will see it as yet another activity he can do "by himself."

A significant advantage of starting at this age is that you will be able to teach bowel and bladder control at the same time. Physical readiness for daytime urinary control usually comes somewhat later than for the bowels. If you begin teaching bowel control when he's younger you will, in effect, end up having to toilet train your child twice. Beginning later will shorten the amount of time you must devote to toilet learning. This in itself will help accomplish one of the ultimate purposes of toilet learning: to free you sooner for other types of creative involvement with your child.

By the time your child is around 2½ your parents and in-laws may be getting impatient. Friends and neighbors may be boasting about how little Tracy, who's about the same age as your son or daughter, has been out of diapers for nearly a year. The older generation will understandably want you to train your child the way they trained theirs. But you can take their tales of when kids were trained in their day, as well as the early ages claimed by well-meaning friends and neighbors, with a grain of salt. Psychologists agree that mothers tend to minimize the age at which their children were trained. Reassure all concerned by explaining that the original reason for early toilet training was the need to do away with the exhausting chore of cleaning diapers. Emphasize that the labor-saving conveniences at your disposal have made it practical for you to begin toilet learning at a time when the child is old enough to handle it quickly and without emotional upset.

Point out that there are drawbacks to early training. For example, as one mother, a doctor's wife who has waited until age 3 to teach all four of her children, pointed out, "The minute a child is out of diapers you've got to know the location of every bathroom in town." Compliment your friends on the achievements of their prodigies, but be strong and don't begin toilet learning until you feel your child is ready. Toilet learning isn't a contest. Its purpose is not to get you and your kid into the *Guinness Book of World Records*. The idea is to teach your child a new skill in a way that enhances her understanding of her body and her world, increases her confidence in herself and her parents, and gives her a sense of independence.

"Many parents in primitive cultures do not seem to understand what investigators mean when they inquire about problems of toilet training," wrote a psychologist, referring to 75 cultures studied, most of which begin bowel training around 2 or later, "for they have experienced no problems of the sort rather typically found in our culture, which makes early demands on a child's power of control."

Waiting till your child is completely ready for toilet learning doesn't necessarily mean more diapers to change. Studies have shown that the older a child is when you begin, the faster the child will learn. So the total number of diapers you'll have to buy, rent, or wash may be the same regardless of when you start. But even if you do have to use diapers a bit longer, the psychological benefits will be worth the extra effort.

The decision that the child is ready for toilet learning should be flexible. You may find that your child has entered one of those phases of negativity that are often a feature of being a 2-year-old, a stage when the child's favorite word is "no." Or, the child may be willing but physically unable to perform. There's no point in trying day after day if you aren't getting results. If after a week or ten days the child doesn't seem to be making progress, it means he was not, in fact, ready after all. Wait a month or so and try again.

Toilet Learning Is an Equal Opportunity Employer

One question remains before preparation for toilet learning can begin: Who is going to teach your child?

In the past, the answer was a foregone conclusion: the mother, of course. Who else?

Studies indicated that, on the average, girls learn elimination control faster than boys. A possible explanation for this discovery may be found in the fact that historically in our society, toilet training has been the mother's job. It seems likely that it's easier for girls to imitate their mothers than for boys. There are many cultures in which this sex division doesn't exist. Among the Ashanti of Ghana, for instance, it's the father who takes a little boy outside to show him how and where to urinate.

It is very important for fathers to become involved in toilet learning and share in teaching both boys and girls. It's especially good for fathers to teach their sons. A father, for one thing, can show a little boy how to urinate standing up.

The little boy's exposure to his father's personality — and vice versa — will be a healthy and positive experience for both.

The child will feel that he's going to the bathroom "just like Daddy." Daddy will recapture an important part of the lost art of fathering sons. A good time to begin a boy's toilet learning is when his father has a vacation, or at least a long weekend. Similarly, the best time to start a girl's toilet learning experience is when her working mother has time off.

The Freud Complex

The most important thing to keep in mind as you approach toilet learning is that it's not all *that* important. Many parents have been led to believe that the way they deal with elimination is uniquely crucial. They worry that if they make one false move in this area of the child's development it will have a permanent effect on his adult personality. Much of this concern arises out of a misunderstanding of the ideas of Dr. Sigmund Freud — and out of Freud's misunderstanding of the process of learning bowel control.

The confusion stems from Freud's book, *Three Contributions to the Theory of Sex*. In it the founder of psychoanalysis said that human sexuality doesn't suddenly arrive at puberty — that it begins to develop in earliest infancy. He said that a baby's immature sexual feeling is first centered on its mouth, and that the satisfaction obtained from sucking is the earliest form of erotic pleasure. Freud theorized that after this "oral phase," children become capable of feeling sexual pleasure from "the activity of the anal zone."

> Children utilizing the erogenous sensitiveness of the anal zone
> can be recognized by their holding back of fecal masses until
> through accumulation there result violent muscular contrac-
> tions; the passage of these masses through the anus is apt to
> produce a marked irritation of the mucous membrane. Besides
> the pain this must produce a sensation of pleasure. One of the
> surest premonitions of later eccentricity or nervousness is
> when an infant obstinately refuses to empty his bowel when
> placed on the chamber by the nurse and reserves this function
> at its own pleasure. It does not concern him that he will soil
> his bed; all he cares for is not to lose the subsidiary pleasure
> while defecating. The educators have again the right inkling
> when they designate children who withhold these functions
> as bad.

Freud went on to suggest that an infant's "holding back of
fecal masses" was a form of masturbation, and — rather aston-
ishingly — that "these masses" were the "precursor" of the penis
as used in anal intercourse. Finally, he said that this "infantile
anal erotism" was eventually transformed into "obstinacy, stin-
giness and orderliness."

Four years later, in a brief paper entitled "Character and Anal
Eroticism," Freud had more to say about this "triad" of the anal
personality. Obstinate, stingy, orderly people, he said,

> took a long time to overcome their infantile fecal inconti-
> nence, and that even in later childhood they suffered from
> isolated failures of this function. As infants, they seemed to
> have belonged to the class who refuses to empty their bowels
> when they are put on the pot because they derive a subsidiary
> pleasure from defecating. . . . From these indications we infer
> that such people are born with a sexual constitution in which
> the erotogenicity of the anal zone is exceptionally strong.

Freud's theories about infant sexuality were extremely influ-
ential. Gradually the notion filtered out to the public that you
could make a child "anal" — even turn a boy into a homo-
sexual — by doing something wrong in toilet training. Some
parents reacted by beginning bowel training extremely early
and with great strictness, to prevent the child from getting used

to the supposedly pleasurable sensation of "anal retention." Others postponed the process as long as possible, in the hope that a permissive approach would avoid provoking the child to resist and thereby learn to enjoy holding back bowel movements.

Sigmund Freud, however, did not believe that neurosis resulted from any act of commission or omission during toilet training. His position was that the anal personality was born, not made. The tendency to derive pleasure from a retained bowel movement was not created by toilet training. It was merely observable while toilet training was in progress. As the child grew up, Freud said, inborn anal sexuality was sublimated in a desire for cleanliness and orderliness (as a reaction to the early desire to play with feces), interest in money (because of the identification of money as dirty — "filthy lucre"), and stubbornness (as a result of the infant's not wanting to part with its stool).

Not only have Freud's ideas about toilet training been misinterpreted, but Freud himself misinterpreted what went on during toilet training. To begin with, to write about "holding back," "obstinately refusing," and "withholding," in an era when bowel training was begun when a child was as young as 1 day, was an absurdity. A child doesn't develop the neuromuscular maturity to move its bowels at will until much, much later. The children Freud was describing as "anal erotics" were not holding back — they were physically unable to perform on command. It is quite likely, in fact, that often the real reason they did not expel the contents of their bowels when "placed on the chamber" (because they were too young to get on it themselves) was that there were no contents to expel. Their parents were trying to catch movements before there were movements to catch.

Freud presumably did not spend a great deal of his time actually observing recalcitrant infants being held over chamber pots. His reports of "obstinate refusals" by children must have come from exasperated parents. Without firsthand knowledge of whether the children in question were neurophysiologically ready to move their bowels at will, it was unscientific for him to have concluded that failure to perform on the pot was "one of the surest premonitions of later eccentricity or nervousness." Perhaps what produced the eccentricity or nervousness was not that the child was born with anal tendencies, but rather that the child was born to impatient, insensitive, demanding, overly critical parents. Freud's own bias against such unfortunate children is evident in his statement that "the educators have again the right inkling when they designate children who withhold these functions as bad." Freud apparently didn't consider the possibility that it was this designating of children as bad that ultimately resulted in neurosis.

Later psychologists attempted to extend Freud's theories to normal children who were not "born with a sexual constitution in which the erotogenicity of the anal zone is exceptionally strong." If parents punished or threatened a child during toilet training, they hypothesized, the pleasure the child would normally get from moving his bowels would be denied him. The child might respond by limiting all pleasure-seeking activities. As the child moved toward adulthood, he might develop a punitive attitude toward himself or toward others. A child's fear of making his parents angry by wetting or soiling could result in the undue concern with neatness, orderliness, and cleanliness which Freud identified with the "anal" personality.

The problem with these speculations is that they looked at toilet training in a vacuum — as if parental punitiveness affected the child deeply if expressed when a child soiled his pants with a bowel movement, but hardly at all when the same child soiled his shirt with grape juice. They failed to consider that it might be the parents' general punitive attitude which produced emotional problems. A child might indeed become compulsively neat and orderly as a result of fear of parental anger at accidents during toilet training — just as the child might become compulsively neat and orderly as a result of fear of parental anger at accidents during finger painting.

The point is that anything about a child that a parent makes much of will have a significant impact on that child's development. The reason that the child's behind has loomed so large to Freudians is that it has loomed so large to parents. If parents start toilet training during the first year and keep it up morning noon and night, day after day, month after month for two years or more, it goes without saying that this interaction will have a profound effect on the child's personality. Of course the child will end up thinking that the main thing that matters in life is "the activities of the anal zone." If parents choose to make the child's toilet habits the focal point of acceptance or rejection, reward or punishment, praise or blame, pride or shame, then the child's ability to control a small number of internal muscles becomes — artificially, arbitrarily, unnecessarily — a crucial factor in determining his adult personality. It is not the anus which has special power over the total psychological and moral development of a human being — it is the parent.

There is a relationship between the technique of toilet education and future character traits, because the way the parent behaves toward the child at this time is typical of the way the parent behaves toward the child all the time. A parent who is warm, accepting, and gentle in teaching the child eating, sleeping, dressing, and playing habits is likely to be warm, accepting, and gentle in teaching the child toilet habits. A parent who is cold, demanding, and abrupt in dealing with a child in general will be cold, demanding, and abrupt in dealing with bowel and bladder control in particular.

Just as children have physical impulses which they must learn to become aware of, understand, and control, parents have psychological impulses — toward anger, toward impatience — that they may not be aware of, that they may not understand, and that they may therefore be unable to control. Toilet learning is a medium through which parents can become vividly aware of how they act toward their children. Toilet learning can have as great a positive influence on parent development as it can on child development.

Preparing Yourself
for Toilet Learning

Before you begin preparing your child for toilet learning, prepare yourself.

In order for a child to learn how to use the toilet, he has to learn to interpret and respond to his internal sensations. In order for you to teach your child, it will be helpful for you to become aware of what you feel in your body when the need for elimination arises. You, of course, have voluntary control over your bowels and your bladder. But your control has become a habit. You no longer need to notice consciously the signals you feel inside. You can prepare for toilet learning by becoming fully aware of these sensations and how you react to them. How do you know that it will shortly be necessary to move your bowels? How do you know that it will very soon be time to urinate?

First, you feel a mild sense of fullness which tells you that you could go if you wanted to — if, for example, you were to start on a long drive. Your response to this feeling is to become alert for more urgent sensations.

This sense of fullness gradually gives way to a feeling of moderate pressure, a mildly unpleasant sensation that you may wish to get rid of by moving your bowels or urinating. But you feel that, if necessary, you could postpone relieving yourself for a short while. The normal muscle tone of your sphincters is enough to counteract the impulse to go to the bathroom.

The moderate pressure soon becomes strong. This is the signal to stop whatever else you are doing and go to the bathroom. Your reaction is to contract your sphincter muscles immediately and keep them that way until you reach the toilet. Practice this tightening and loosening several times to experience what you will be asking your child to do when you ask him to "hold it in."

If for some reason you are delayed in getting to a toilet, the feeling of strong pressure becomes unpleasant and extremely urgent. You must powerfully use your voluntary control over your sphincters in order to resist this feeling. You are concerned that your voluntary control may not be strong enough. You feel that if for any reason you could not get to the toilet in time, your involuntary muscles might take over and force you to relieve yourself.

When you get to the toilet, it's not enough simply to "let go" — you must actively push to get the flow started. You should become familiar with this maneuver because 2½-year-olds may have difficulty beginning urinary release and it's helpful to know what they're going through. Once urination has begun, the bladder more or less empties itself. Only at the end is it necessary to contract the bladder several times in order to expel the last few drops. Note that you don't "push" to do this — you "squeeze." In fact, the maneuver you use is remarkably similar to the one you use to hold in.

To move your bowels, you bear down, not just with your abdominal muscles, but with your lungs too. You do this by taking a short breath, closing your epiglottis — the flap of cartilage which closes off the voice box when you swallow — and contracting your chest muscles. This is known in medical terminology as "Valsalva's maneuver." The air pressure in your lungs increases the pressure on the descending colon, helping it to control and empty its contents. You perform the same Valsalva's maneuver when you clear your throat or grunt. That's why, in many primitive cultures, parents grunt to show their children how to use the internal muscles to empty their bowels.

Finally there's the feeling of relief that the bowels and bladder are at last being emptied, and that no further attention will have to be paid to them for a while.

Your child feels exactly the same sensations that you do. But there's one critical difference: he doesn't know how to interpret or respond to them yet. Once you've become aware of the progression of sensations in yourself, you'll be better able to understand what's going on inside your child as he learns the correct interpretation and response. A parent who gets impatient with a child who's trying to learn how to use the toilet hasn't recognized the extreme complexity of this internal process. The best way of becoming an understanding parent is to constantly put yourself in the child's place.

Preparing Your Child for Toilet Learning

Before you present Part 2 of this book to your child, you should prepare him by teaching him to recognize — and tell you about — the sensations he feels. Until now, the child has taken elimination for granted. Your role at this point is to express your awareness of this process. After a while, the child, knowing that his bodily functions are of interest to you, will begin to draw your attention to them.

As your child approaches readiness for toilet learning, he will pass through three stages of development:

1) HAS WET: First, he becomes aware that he has just had a bowel movement or urinated.
2) IS WETTING: Second, he becomes aware that he's in the middle of a bowel movement or of urination.
3) WILL WET: Third, he becomes aware that he will soon move his bowels or urinate.

These stages may appear at almost any time between the child's first and third birthdays, and may last for days, weeks, or months. The trick is for you to identify the stage which your child is at, and to encourage him to move along to the next.

Has Wet

Begin preparing your child for toilet learning by teaching him to recognize the sensations that follow elimination and to put them into words. When you sense that he has gone in his diaper, ask him to tell you whether he urinated, moved his bowels, or both. Tell the child that from now on he is going to let you know when he needs to be changed.

This is the time for you to decide what words you want your child to learn. The words "wee-wee" and "doo-doo" are printed in the text of Part 2. I don't hold any special brief for these particular words, except that they seem to have stood the test of time, and no kindergarten teacher ever washed out a child's mouth with soap for saying them in front of the principal. If you prefer other words, feel free to substitute them when reading the text to your child. "BM," "doody," "ka-ka," "poo-poo," "sissy," "wet," "pee" — all are fine. Some parents use "make potty" or "go" to refer to both functions, but it's helpful to have a word for each substance. Since the methods of control differ, it's important for you to be able to refer to each one separately. The basis for your choice should be, "What words do I want to hear myself and my child say for the next few years?" I know one mother who taught her daughter to call moving her bowels "making a yucky." This could grate on one's ears after a while, and it suggests a feeling of disgust that's unnecessary for good hygiene. It's best to choose words that are common among your child's playmates. Not too many parents really want their kid going around saying, "I have to defecate."

There can, in fact, be a danger in using "grown-up" words that the child may not understand. Typical of the cases which have been reported is that of a Brooklyn, New York, boy who devel-ped a "toilet phobia" at the age of 27 months. He became terrified to go near the contraption for fear of falling in. He was sure there was a lion inside the bowl, waiting to eat him up. The child was brought to a psychiatrist, who discovered that the parents had recently begun using the word "urine" in the child's training. Whenever they said "urine," the child heard "you're in!"

Whatever words you choose, its a good idea to be consistent: don't vary the words you use to refer to the same substance. Use the words you've selected whenever you discover that your child has gone in his diaper. When you check and see that he's wet you can say, "Jason made wee-wee." While you are changing him you might say, "Jason made doo-doo, see?" The idea is for the child to learn that there are two distinctive substances that come out of him, each of which has its own name. Soon the child will begin to say, "Daddy, I made wee-wee!"

Is Wetting

Next, the child learns to recognize the sensations that go with the act of elimination. Be observant: when you see by the child's facial expression or posture that he's straining to move his bowels, say, "Jason is making doo-doo." When Mommy is urinating, the thing to say to your little girl is, "Look, Jennifer, Mommy is making wee-wee." In short order your child will be announcing, "Mommy, I'm making doo-doo!"

Will Wet

Next comes the third developmental stage — the one in which the child can let you know in advance. Part 2 of this book includes the suggestion to the child that he tell you beforehand when he has to go. So when he starts to do this, you can begin to present Part 2 to your child.

Guide to Part 2

Part 2 of this book is an illustrated learning program designed for you to narrate to your child. Its purpose is twofold. First, it will tell you when your child is ready to begin toilet learning. By observing the level of your child's comprehension and interest as you present Part 2 to her, you will be able to decide whether she has reached the stage of development at which your efforts and hers will be worthwhile. Then, when you feel that your child is ready, Part 2 will help you teach her.

Part 2 consists of pictures showing the steps in toilet learning, and a script to guide you in explaining the meaning of each picture and encouraging your child to do what is being shown. You may read the text as it appears, or talk to the child in your own words, using the text as a point of departure.

Before you begin to read and show Part 2 to your child, this guide will familiarize you with every step in toilet learning. It is keyed to each page in Part 2 so that the function of the text and illustrations will be clear to you.

The first time you present Part 2 to your child, do it in a

comfortable place that's free from distractions. If while you're reading the child says she wants to go into the bathroom, so much the better, because that's exactly what you are trying to teach her to do. After the child has had a chance to explore the bathroom, you can continue reading the book together there as you point out and demonstrate the various fixtures. If the child does not ask to visit the bathroom while you are presenting Part 2, you can take her there afterward and ask her to name each of its features and show and tell you how they're used.

As you read each page, point to the picture so the child will know where to look. You can explain what the picture shows in as much detail as you think necessary. For example, after you read the text on page 74 you can point to the picture in the center and say, "Look — the mother is putting a clean diaper on the baby so the baby will be nice and dry."

Part 2 shows toilet learning as a part of the child's daily activities, and many everyday objects are shown. Encourage the child to name and point to familiar things in each picture, such as the blocks on page 105 and the car on page 100.

Judge how much your child understands by asking questions about the pictures as you go along. For example, once you have shown the picture of the mother wearing underpants to the child (page 75) you can point to the picture below and ask. "What is Daddy wearing?" After presenting page 88 ("Firemen go to the bathroom") you could ask, "Why is the fireman sitting on the toilet?"

If the child isn't able to answer your questions in a way that suggests that she's getting the drift of what the pictures are showing and what she's supposed to do, let the whole matter of toilet learning drop for a while. Let the child keep the book and encourage her to "read" it on her own. Allow a month or so to go by and then go over Part 2 with her again. Remember that if the child isn't ready to understand Part 2, the child isn't ready to learn how to use the toilet.

Presenting Part 2 to your child will take about 15 minutes. If your child gets restless, say "Okay — that's all for now. We'll read this book again later." When you return to the book later in the day, leaf quickly through the pages you've already covered to refresh the child's memory.

The process of toilet learning may take a few weeks or it may continue for months. Part 2 should be presented to your child as often as you wish during this time — every day or two at first, less frequently as the child makes progress. If there's an older child in the house, ask the brother or sister to help by going over the book with the younger child. In addition to smoothing and speeding toilet learning, this will encourage a more cooperative relationship between your children.

If your child is usually cared for during the day by some-one besides you — in a day care setting, for example, or by a housekeeper or relative — you may wish the care-giver to help in toilet learning. Ask the care-giver to become familiar with Part 1 and to present Part 2 to the child.

Now, as you are about to present Part 2 to your child for the first time, remember: *Relax*. Act as if toilet learning is the most natural thing in the world — because it is.

*

Page 63:
Look — the little girl is playing. She's having fun. She feels nice and dry in her diaper.

The first page of Part 2 shows a child playing, because this is what your child usually will be doing when she discovers that she has gone in her diapers. You emphasize how pleasant it is to be dry. The sex of the child in the picture has purposely been made ambiguous. Depending on the sex of your child, you may wish to describe the child on this page and the two that follow as a girl or a boy.

Page 64:
Uh-oh! The little girl just went in her diaper! She feels wet and sticky. She doesn't look happy, does she? Being wet and sticky

*in your diaper doesn't feel good, does it? You like to feel nice
and dry.*

You want to remind your child constantly how uncomfortable it is not to have control, and how comfortable it will be to have it. The best motivation to encourage in your child is the desire to do away with the unpleasant feeling of being wet and sticky. Even the tiniest infant wails when the urine in her wet diaper becomes cold, and stops when the diaper's changed. Children do become used to the discomfort of being wet. But just because they tolerate chafing and itching doesn't mean they like it. Your first role in toilet learning is to help your child become fully aware that she'd rather be dry.

Praise your child generously when she makes progress at any stage of toilet learning. But it's not a good idea to teach your child that the main reason she should control her body is to please other people, as in "Eat your oatmeal for Mommy." One book went off the deep end in promoting other-directedness by suggesting that parents tell their children that if they perform on the toilet, "the Cookie Monster will be happy." This is supposed to be clever infant psychology. But what happens to the child's value system when she discovers that the Cookie Monster is just a puppet? Even worse, what happens if the child is slow to learn, or has an "accident"? Is she to feel that she has let down you, Grandma, and/or the Cookie Monster? Would such feelings of guilt speed up toilet learning? It's far more likely that they'd slow it down.

The same book suggested that mothers systematically use treats such as candy and ice cream as a reward for getting it in the pot. This "behavior modification" method was originally developed for toilet training institutionalized retarded adults with whom all other attempts had reportedly failed. To suggest that parents stuff kids with sweets in order to get them to go to the bathroom is very foolish. "Two weeks after an unsuccessful training attempt," wrote a newspaper columnist who tried this method, "my 2-year-old is still begging for candy. I would rather have her wearing diapers than either whining or rotting out her teeth." You don't want to teach your child to expect a material reward simply for taking care of her bodily needs. The authors of this book were promoting the use of "rat psychology" on children because they put a premium on instant results — so-called "toilet training in less than a day." Even if lightning results were easily obtainable — and an Indiana State University study found that they were not — they wouldn't be desirable. It's not good child psychology to make a child feel that behavior which has been acceptable for years has suddenly become intolerable. The Indiana State study showed that when this high-pressure method was used, kids developed temper tantrums that interfered with learning toilet control. All mothers interviewed "reported fits of crying and screaming in varying degrees the first few times their child was mandatorily required to sit on the potty . . . numerous tantrums — sitting down, hitting, and running away from the mothers — were reported. . . . All the mothers expressed bewilderment and frustration over how to handle the child."

Aside from the normal amount of praise which you would give your child whenever she behaves in a way of which you approve, the child's only reward for success in toilet learning should be the pleasure of being dry — and her own sense of accomplishment.

Page 65:
We will show you what to do so you can feel nice and dry. Let's sit down and learn from this book.

Both mother and father should present Part 2 to the child. They should do it together whenever possible, taking turns if necessary.

Page 66:
What's in your diaper comes out of you.

This seemingly obvious fact has to be explained. The child has seldom, if ever, actually seen either substance come out.

37

Page 67:

Part of the food you eat comes out of you. Look — people eating.

The mystery of just exactly what these strange substances are should be cleared up once and for all.

Pages 68 and 69:

The food you eat is made into
Bones to make you big
Teeth to chew with
Hair to comb
Nails to cut
And big strong muscles to play with.

Far from knowing why they urinate and defecate, most children this age don't even have the slightest idea why they've got to *eat!*

Page 70:

Anything you don't need goes out of you. (See the wee-wee coming out of the dog?)

The chances are good that your child has seen dogs urinate more often than she has seen people do so. Before as well as during toilet learning, when neighborhood pets are relieving themselves, you can draw her attention to what they're doing.

Page 71:

One of the things that comes out of you is wet. We call it wee-wee. See the rain puddle? Rain is wet.

Before you introduce Part 2 to the child, you've already taught her the words you'll use in toilet learning. (See page 31.) This is a good time to review them. If you plan to use different words from those printed in the text accompanying Part 2, feel free to substitute the ones you wish to teach as you read to your child.

Page 72:

The other thing that comes out of you is sticky. We call it doo-doo. (See the horse making doo-doo?)

It's natural for children to want to touch and smell their BMs. They want to know what those remarkable, pungent brown lumps their bodies seem to be manufacturing are. There was even a time shortly after World War II when child psychologists thought it was a good idea for parents to encourage their children to play with feces. This was an overreaction to the excessive concern with cleanliness of the early twentieth century. But somewhere between making a child feel that fecal matter is disgusting, and smiling proudly as a child creates artistic projects with it, there ought to be a happy medium.

You may have strong feelings of disgust at feces, left over from your own toilet training. This revulsion, in turn, was left over from an age before indoor plumbing. Teaching disgust at feces in those days was an important way of preventing the spread of infection. Improved sanitation has reduced the importance of fecal matter in the spread of disease, and has done away with the need to teach children a horror of their own bodily products. A mild aversion, plus good hygiene, will suffice. So if your aversion is more than mild, try not to pass it on to your child.

At the same time, it's important to allow kids to explore fully the feeling of being messy and dirty. The opportunity for plenty of play with finger paints, clay, and good old-fashioned garden-variety dirt will soon do away with the desire to play with bowel movements.

Page 73:

When wee-wee and doo-doo are in your diaper, they make you feel wet and sticky. You don't like it. You want to feel nice and dry. When you were little, if you were wet and sticky, you had to call for Mommy and Daddy to help you.

You suggest the immaturity of having to depend on grown-ups to be changed. Though your child is now just as dependent as the child in the illustration, you talk as if this stage is already a thing of the past.

The words "Mommy" and "Daddy" are printed in the text of Part 2. If different words are used in your family, substitute them as you read the narration to your child.

Page 74:
You wore diapers. We had to change you, so you could feel nice and dry.

Long before toilet learning begins, try to make a point of changing the child cheerfully. It's a bad idea to give to the child the impression that there is something disgusting or dirty about the products of her body, or that you don't like having to change her.

One way of beginning to establish the fact that bowel movements belong in the toilet is to let the child watch you empty the BM from the diaper into the bowl, and to allow her to flush afterwards.

Page 75:
Soon you're going to wear underpants.
Just like Mommy.
Just like Daddy.

As soon as the child attains some degree of control of her bowels, you can put her in training pants (which we'd like to see called *learning* pants) during the daytime. Use the thick, absorbent kind, such as Carter's,* because in the beginning, getting it in the toilet will be an "accident." Wearing training pants is good because the child immediately feels that something is different about herself. She looks different. Training pants go on and off differently from diapers. They are made of different material. Wearing them will remind the child of the importance of control.

---

* William Carter Co., Needham Heights, Mass. 02194.

You don't want the child to feel that she's being pressured into staying dry by the fear of soiling her clothes through the training pants. If the child seems worried about wetting her pants or clothes, reassure her that if she does, it's okay — just part of learning. If she still seems concerned, put the child back in diapers until her confidence builds. The same goes if you are concerned. If you find that discovering soiled training pants irritates you, it's better to stay with diapers for the time being.

You call the training pants "underpants" because you want to emphasize their similarity to what everybody else in her family wears. You point out that underpants are what Mommy and Daddy wear because your child naturally wants to be like you. Calling the training pants underpants makes the child feel that she's moving on to grown-up clothing and is therefore expected to develop grown-up toilet habits. When you give your child "underpants" like yours, it will be an expression of your confidence in her ability. Your child will want to be worthy of your confidence and try as hard as possible not to mess them up. When the child inevitably does, don't scold. Say matter-of-factly, "Look — you went in your underpants. It made you feel wet and sticky, like when you used to wear diapers. From now on, let's do it in the toilet so you can feel nice and dry."

At first, use the largest size of training pants that will stay up and not leave a gap around the legs. You want them to be as easy to pull up and down as possible. Once the child learns to handle the mechanics of getting them on and off, you can go to a smaller size.

Page 76:
When you feel like you've got to make wee-wee or doo-doo, you will help yourself by going to the bathroom.

Emphasize that the time to arrive in the bathroom is before anything happens.

Rather than using the word "you" as you read to your child about what she's going to do, you may wish to insert her name in the text. For example, "When Lori feels like she's got to

41

make wee-wee or doo-doo, she will help herself by going to the bathroom."

Pages 76 and 77:
In the bathroom there's a toilet. The toilet is there so nobody in our home has to be wet and sticky. We put our wee-wee and doo-doo in the toilet.
> *The toilet is round.*
> *It has water in it.*
> *It has a seat that goes up and down.*
> *It has a cover.*

If you want to teach your child to use a word other than "toilet," substitute it as you read the text.

If the child is able to sit comfortably on the adult toilet after a few tries, it's a good idea to teach her to use it from the beginning. If the child has difficulty climbing on or off, build or buy a low, sturdy step with a wide, deep tread and show the child how to put it in position.* If the child finds it hard to balance on the toilet seat, a training seat — let's re-name it: a learning seat — that fits over the toilet can be used.† If the child feels more comfortable on a learning seat, take it with you when you and the child are away from home, or keep a second one in the trunk of the car.

Those who've recommended that kids always learn to use a potty first were talking about younger children, who were much

---

* Excellent folding step stool and chair combinations are manufactured by Peter Pan, 649 39th St., Brooklyn, N.Y. 11232; Worldbest, 212 Elm St., New Canaan, Conn. 06840; Mapes, 130 Cuttermill Rd., Great Neck, N.Y. 11021; Gem, Box 306, Bascom, Ohio 44809.
† The Secondary Trainer Seat made by Kiddie, Avon, Mass. 02322, has no back or arms. It's a tot-sized version of the adult toilet seat, onto which it snaps. A similar unit, the Model 150W, is made by Peterson, 6904 Tujunga Ave., N. Hollywood, Calif. 91605. The "Little Guys" training seat by Sybar, 5935 W. Irving Park Rd., Chicago, Ill. 60634, fits securely under the adult seat.

Kiddie Products also manufactures the Trainer Seat with arms and a back, molded from one piece of plastic. Similar seats include the Model 9550, by Century, 2150 W. 114th St., Cleveland, Ohio 44106; and the Model 525W by Peterson. Kewaunee, Box 186, Kewaunee, Wis. 54216, manufactures the Model 711TC, which has arms and a back. It's made of wood and metal and weighs four pounds — nearly three times as much as the plastic seats with arms and backs. Unlike those seats, however, the 711TC folds flat for travel or storage.

too small to sit on an adult toilet. In those days, infants were required to spend hours on the pot, waiting for something to come out. So of course they needed a throne of their own. A few pages farther on there's a picture that shows the child what a potty is and how it's used. But if your child can sit comfortably on the toilet now, you may not want to get her used to an appliance from which she'll only have to be "weaned" later.

If your child is not comfortable and securely balanced on the toilet, or has difficulty getting on and off, or if you just feel that little kids and potties go together, you can teach her how to use the potty. But in any event, the child should be shown the toilet first. The child will be more interested in using the potty if she feels that it's her own "little toilet," just like Mommy and Daddy's big toilet. When you use the toilet, you can encourage your child to practice using the potty alongside you — a pants-down dry run, with no results expected. Also, since the child will need to be capable of going to the bathroom where no potty is available — restaurants, gas stations, relatives' houses — it is better for the child's first exposure to a toilet be at home rather than, say, in a busy restaurant washroom. And the child who learns first to go in a potty should understand what a toilet is, because that's where the little pot is emptied.

Page 78:
Before you use the toilet you pull your pants down all the way.

Make sure that your child's trousers are as loose at the waist as possible, with only elastic holding them up — no buttons, snaps, or zippers. Clothing which is difficult to remove is a major cause of accidents. If you begin during the warm months of the year, you can let the child wear just training pants around the house. Once she can handle the training pants, add the trousers.

Pages 78 and 79:
Little girls sit on the toilet when they make wee-wee and doo-doo . . .
Just like Mommy.

A study of child-rearing practices of American mothers observed that "generally speaking, modesty taboos prevent American children from learning their toilet habits in the way they learn many other prescribed forms of behavior — by imitation." By adopting an open-door policy when you use the bathroom, you can accelerate your child's progress in toilet learning. Young children love to imitate their parents and their older brothers and sisters.

If you feel comfortable letting your child watch you, give a play-by-play so she can follow each step of what you are doing: "I'm going to make a doo-doo. First I pull my pants down. Then I sit down . . . and squeeze like this . . . ."

Kids find it easier to balance on the adult toilet if they hold on to both sides of the toilet seat, as shown in the illustration.

If your little girl insists on trying to urinate standing up, "just like Daddy," don't stop her — she'll only try it on the sly when you're not looking. Let her take a shot at it. She'll soon discover her equipment doesn't work that way, and that'll be the end of that.

Page 80:
Little boys stand in front of the toilet when they make wee-wee.

Girls should know how boys do it, boys should know how girls do it, but each should learn to do it his or her own way. Teaching a boy to urinate while standing is advantageous because it brings more imitative energy into action. A little boy wants to do things like his father does them. When boys were trained before they could stand by themselves, naturally they first learned to urinate sitting down. Eventually they graduate to doing it from a standing position. When toilet learning is begun around 2½, however, there's no reason why a little boy who's tall enough can't be taught to urinate standing up almost from the start. As you show the toilet to a boy, encourage him to try a dry run standing up, "just like Daddy."

At first, when a boy comes to you and says he has to make a wee-wee, you won't be sure whether he's got his functions and their names straight. When in doubt, he should sit on the toilet regardless of whether he claims he wants to move his bladder or bowels. But as his predictions become trustworthy, when he says he wants to urinate, suggest that he begin doing it standing up. Little boys like to steady themselves by holding on to the rim of the toilet bowl, so make sure it's kept especially clean.

Children often have difficulty letting go when they need to urinate. To start the stream at will it's necessary for the child to be able to use her lungs and her abdominal muscles to direct internal pressure onto the neck of the bladder, which stimulates the bladder to contract. This maneuver is just as complicated as it sounds, and children need plenty of time to learn it. Often, the more they "push," the harder they hold in. If this happens, tell the child to "just relax and wait a few minutes and the wee-wee will come out all by itself." This would be a good time to review Part 2 with your child. Listening to you and looking at the pictures can distract the child enough for the urinary release mechanism to work by itself.

The father should explain to his son, and a mother should explain to her daughter, how to squeeze out the last few drops of urine.

Pages 80 and 81:
and sit when they make doo-doo . . .
  Just like Daddy.

A young child is so used to moving his bowels without thinking about it that when he's called upon to move them consciously, he may not know which muscles to use. Since defecating and grunting both utilize Valsalva's maneuver (see pages 28–29), you can give your child an idea of what he's supposed to do by grunting and asking that he imitate you.

Page 82:
Brian makes wee-wee and doo-doo in a potty which is like a little toilet.

If you plan to use a potty, describe the picture as follows: "You are going to use a potty which is like a little toilet, just like this little boy is doing."

45

You emphasize the similarity between the potty your child uses and the toilet you use in order to build on the child's desire to imitate you. It's better, for this reason, to use a potty that looks like an adult toilet.*

Don't use the urine deflector supplied with most potties. It might hurt a little boy as he climbs on or off. Besides, you want to teach him how to direct his stream downward.

Many potties are equipped with a strap to hold the child down. Strapping a youngster in has no place in toilet learning. The child should feel that the reason she's on the toilet is that she wants to be there — not that she has to be. Often the same parent who considers it necessary to strap a child into a potty chair considers it unnecessary to strap a child into an automobile safety seat.

The best place for the potty is in the bathroom. If at first the child has difficulty holding it in till she gets to the bathroom, you could begin toilet learning with the potty in the room where the child plays. But the goal is for the child to go into the bathroom just like his parents and older brothers and sisters. Putting the potty there will make the most of the child's desire to imitate.

A second potty kept in the trunk of the car will be helpful in emergencies. One advantage of the type of potty with a

* Such as the "Baby Toilette" by Cosco, 2525 State St., Columbus, Ind. 47201; the Model 132 by Pride-Trimble, Box 450, Southern Pines, N.C. 28387; the Model 9710 by Century, 2150 W. 114th St., Cleveland, Ohio 44106; the Model 77W by Peterson, 6904 Tujunga Ave., N. Hollywood, Calif. 91605; and "First Years Toilet" by Kiddie, Avon, Mass. 02322. The Pride-Trimble, Century, and Kiddie units have the virtue of a detachable seat with arms which snaps onto the adult toilet, for use as a learning seat when the child is ready to progress.
Century also makes the Model 9830PG, which contains a music box that plays "How Dry I Am" when the child deposits something in the bowl. A similar unit, the Model 79Y by Peterson, features a built-in tissue dispenser. These units cost several dollars more than the average potty, but your child may enjoy the gimmick.
The following units don't resemble toilets but fold handily into step stools that kids can use when they progress to the adult toilet: Model 750PS by Kewaunee, Box 186, Kewaunee, Wis. 54216; Model 675 by Taylor-Tot, Box 636, Frankfort, Ky. 40601.
These potty chairs don't look like grown-up toilets either, but fold flat for travel or storage: Model 4040 by Worldbest, 212 Elm St., New Canaan, Conn. 06840; Model 4001 by Delta, 1270 Fulton St., Brooklyn, N.Y. 11216; Nursery Training Seat by Bunny Bear, Everett, Mass. 02149; Model 741PS by Kewaunee

removable top that doubles as a learning seat is that when you are on the road or visiting, you can snap off the seat and use it over a toilet, saving you the trouble of washing out the potty's bowl.

It's been suggested that the child be taught to empty the potty. This is not a good idea. Sooner or later the child will drop the bowl or spill its contents, make a mess and feel that she has failed. Why require the child to perform a balancing act that, as soon as she begins to use the adult toilet, she'll have no need for? All parents hope for the day when their children will be able to go to the bathroom completely on their own. But nearly all kids are going to need help of some kind for a long time — with their clothes, with wiping. As long as you have to be in the room, you might as well empty the potty and save yourself some aggravation.

Page 82:
After you go, you take toilet paper and wipe yourself so you'll be nice and clean. Then you drop the paper in the toilet.

Is there a youngster who hasn't pulled half the toilet paper off the roll, just to see how much there is? Show your child how to pull it off without unrolling too much, how to tear off a few sheets, wipe, and drop the paper in the toilet. Some children immediately learn how to wipe themselves, while others need help with this part of toilet learning until they are 5 or older. Many kids who are able to wipe themselves still need to be reminded to do so. If your child has a hard time wiping herself, continue to help her.

The fact that girls wipe from the front after urinating can be confusing to a younger brother. I know one little boy who after watching his older sister on the toilet, tried to wipe himself from the front after a BM.

Page 83:
When you're all done, you get off the toilet and pull your pants up. Then you pull the handle on the toilet and make it go "Whoosh!"

At first, guide your child's hands to teach her how to wipe, pull her pants up, and flush the toilet. From then on, let the child perform these motions without much help from you. Resist the impulse to do things for your child out of impatience. Take your time and let the child practice these movements until she can handle them confidently by herself.

Children sometimes have a hard time pulling their trousers up because their buttocks stick out. To make it easier, teach your child to bend her knees slightly while raising her pants. She should place one hand behind her back, palm facing backward under the waistband, and pull the waistband up in front with the other hand. Practice in pulling pants down and up can begin before toilet learning. If the child is already capable of dressing and undressing herself, toilet learning will be easier.

The noise of flushing may bother some kids. For this reason it has been suggested that children should leave the bathroom after they're wiped, and that the parent should flush the toilet with the door closed. A more sensible approach is to encourage the child to get used to the sound of the toilet being flushed before she begins depositing anything in the bowl. It's common for a child to discover as soon as she's able to stand that she can make the big shiny thing in that funny little room go whoosh if she pulls the shiny little handle. Don't stop a toddler from playing like this unless she's getting really obsessive about it. It's great practice for later on.

Another reason for the suggestion of flushing behind closed doors is concern that a child may feel insulted that after all the work she has gone through to put a BM in the toilet, the parent would immediately get rid of it. But ideally, the parent shouldn't be doing the flushing. If the mother or father pulls the handle the child may feel that the product of her efforts has been rejected by the parent. As child psychoanalyst Anna Freud put it, "Children find it easier to be active themselves in throwing out their own highly cathected [emotionally charged] body products than be deprived of them passively." If, however, your child finds the noise of the toilet disturbing, you can wait until she has left the room to flush, preferably with the door open.

Be ready to comfort her if she finds the idea upsetting that something that has come out of her is going down the drain.

Pages 84 and 85:
In the city, the wee-wee and doo-doo go out of the toilet into a big pipe, underneath the ground.

Another way of preventing fear of flushing the toilet is to show the child what happens after the handle is pulled, which is done in these pages.

You can show your child manholes and explain that some of them are openings so that people can go down and fix the big pipe where the wee-wee and doo-doo go.

Pages 86 and 87:
In the country the wee-wee and doo-doo go out of the toilet right into the ground.

You can stop at a construction site where new houses are being built, and show the child an excavation for a septic tank.

Pages 88 through 95:
Everybody goes to the bathroom.
Firemen go to the bathroom.
Policemen go to the bathroom.
Babysitters go to the bathroom.
People on TV go to the bathroom.
The mailman goes to the bathroom.
Grandpa goes to the bathroom.
Doctors go to the bathroom.
Grandma goes to the bathroom.

You emphasize the universality and maturity of toilet learning. The child, who wants to be like a grown-up, sees that all adults have learned how to use the toilet. Going to the bathroom is not a strange activity that goes on only in her house. Everyone does it.

Pages 96 and 97:
After they are all done on the toilet, they wash their hands so they'll be nice and clean.
   Just like you.

The child is shown that cleanliness too is a sign of maturity.

Pages 98 through 100:
Almost everywhere you go there are bathrooms.
   In a restaurant . . .
   in a gas station there are bathrooms.

The child sees that her house isn't the only place in the world that has a toilet. You point out other places where she'll be going to the bathroom.

Get the child used to the idea of going to the bathroom outside the home by taking her with you into bathrooms in public places even when she doesn't need to relieve herself. The child should not encounter her first black horseshoe-shaped toilet seat when she's in a rush to go.

In the past, it was often assumed that when the whole family was out together, it was the mother's job to take the kids to the bathroom, little boys included. It's a much better idea for the father to take his son to the men's room.

Page 101:
There's a bathroom in a plane . . .
In a big boat . . .
In a train . . .
In a big bus . . .

Children at this age are often fascinated with vehicles of every kind, especially big ones that go fast and make lots of noise. The knowledge that there are bathrooms in planes and trains will make going to the one at home seem a little less ordinary to the child. A child may enjoy making believe that she's "going to the bathroom in a big boat."

When you're traveling by plane, train, or intercity bus, it's a good idea to show the child the bathroom before she needs to go. The child may clutch if she has to cope simultaneously with urgent sensations and a strange, cramped, lurching water closet — however exciting the idea of mobile bathrooms may seem.

Page 102:
There are bathrooms at the zoo.

The zoo is a good place to take a child during toilet learning because it provides an opportunity for the child to see that all animals relieve themselves, not just the neighborhood dogs and cats.

Page 104:
Sometimes when you're outside you've got to make wee-wee or doo-doo. If there's no bathroom, you can make wee-wee and doo-doo on the ground, like all the animals do. Look — the deer is making wee-wee in the woods.

You should plant in the child's mind the idea that in a pinch she can go in the bushes. Otherwise you may find yourself in the car miles from a bathroom with a child who has been pro-grammed to go nowhere but in a proper toilet, but has only a limited ability to hold it in. It's a good idea to take the child on a practice walk in the woods when she's about due to relieve herself, and give her a chance to do it on the ground. This way you can avoid a panic if the child has to go badly and you have no time to show her what to do. Remember to show the child how to cover her BM like a good scout. Always keep a supply of tissues in your car, just in case.

Page 105:
From now on, when you feel like you want to make wee-wee or doo-doo, don't go in your underpants. Hold it in as hard as you can, and come to Daddy and Mommy. Say, "I want to go to the bathroom." We will take you there.

Encourage your child to come to you when she needs to go to the bathroom — but don't rely on her to do it at first. If her behavior gives you a hint that she has to go — if, for instance, she begins to tug at her pants or shift from foot to foot — ask if she wants to go to the bathroom. Make a special point of reminding the child before she leaves the house, takes a nap, and goes to bed. Remember, though, that a young child feels the need to urinate only when the bladder is completely full — so be understanding if the child has to go minutes after saying she doesn't.

Every time the child comes to you saying she wants to go, let a pat or a smile show that you are pleased. At first the child may proudly signal you after she has gone. Don't scold: this is progress. If the child has already made a bowel movement by the time she reaches the toilet, let her see you empty it into the toilet.

Don't pop your cork if the child can't go while sitting on the toilet but wets her pants a few minutes later. Most children don't become physically able to start urinating when the bladder is only partly full until some time between the ages of 3½ and 6.

During the first stages of toilet learning, take the child to the bathroom and encourage her as she tries to use the toilet. When she's handling everything smoothly, suggest that now she can go there all by herself. Stay within earshot in case she needs help.

Page 106:
"Daddy," the little boy says, "Sometimes I can't hold it in till I get to the bathroom."

"That's okay," says the Daddy. "If you go in your underpants, don't worry. Just tell us so we can give you nice dry clothes. Soon you'll be able to hold it in better and better."

Toilet learning is a good time to develop the patience you will need to help your child grow in the years to come. The most effective policy to adopt toward your child's progress in toilet learning is to praise hits and reassure after misses.

Be matter-of-fact about accidents. Say, "Jeremy, you made

wee-wee in your pants. Next time try to do it in the toilet, okay?" Don't call him a bad boy, and swallow that tsk. Scolding, anger, and punishment are absolutely out of the question — whether for not learning "fast enough," or for accidents. Punishing a child for misbehavior within her control can be a legitimate child-rearing technique. But accidents are precisely that: accidental — outside the child's control — and must be accepted cheerfully. Punishment has been proven to interfere with the acquisition of new skills, and has no place in toilet learning.

Children who are learning control often become upset when they go in their pants. They may be unpleasantly surprised by the quick onrush of sensations. They may be angry at themselves for having fumbled a chance to demonstrate their new skill to themselves or to you. Far from benefiting from punishment at such a moment, the child runs the risk of punishing herself excessively. When a child cries after an accident she needs all the parental support she can get. A hug at a time like this will be far more productive than a harsh word.

You may find that the child quickly learns the concept of bowel control, but continues to have urinary lapses. This is perfectly normal. Bowel movements are easier to hold back. They're less frequent, and the child must strain to get them out. If she consciously chooses not to push, the movement stays in, at least temporarily. The bladder, in comparison, empties automatically whenever it's full if the child doesn't know how to hold in. It's harder for the child to stop something from happening than to decide not to make something happen.

Some authors have recommended that bowel control be taught first, followed by bladder control. Again, they were talking about training younger children. One of the main advantages of waiting until your child is totally ready for toilet learning is that she will often be physically capable of learning both forms of control at the same time. If you start the child on Part 2 and find that she soon learns to control her bowels, but can't seem to hold in urine, don't push the urinary side of toilet learning. Wait a month or so and then present Part 2 to the child again, this time emphasizing bladder control.

53

Even after a child has good urinary control there will be occasional lapses when she's involved in play or is tired. The arrival of cooler weather, a visitor in the home, a slight cold, or excitement about a trip may result in accidents. A move to a new home or the arrival of a new baby can cause a child to revert. When the child is going through a period in which she's learning a large number of words, toilet habits can be temporarily "forgotten." These occasional regressions are not bad — in fact, they're quite healthy. "The capacity to function on a high level of achievement," Anna Freud wrote, "is in itself no guarantee that the performance will be stable: on the contrary, it is more normal for the child, and a better guarantee for later mental health if, during the state of growth, he reverts occasionally to more infantile modes of behavior before these are abandoned."

Other progress, such as vocabulary, may be suspended temporarily as toilet skills are learned. Sometimes, as the child learns to control bowels and bladder, disturbances may crop up in seemingly unconnected areas — fussiness in eating, temper tantrums, difficulty in sleeping. If such problems do arise, it's a good idea to suspend toilet learning for a few weeks. When it's resumed, it should be at an especially gentle pace, with careful observation of the child's behavior in other areas.

When the child has an accident she may get discouraged and ask to be put in a diaper. Try to talk her out of it by assuring her that she's learning to hold her wee-wee in and soon she'll be able to keep her underpants dry all the time. If she insists, let her wear a diaper for the rest of that day. The following morning the chances are she'll let you put her in underpants as if nothing had happened.

Occasionally, a sudden regression in day or night urinary control can be a warning signal of a urinary infection, an especially common ailment in girls. This is particularly likely if the child also seems irritable, is eating poorly, vomits, runs a temperature, urinates frequently, voids urine that has an unusual odor, or cries or complains of pain on urination. One of the symptoms of a urinary infection is "urgency" — the sudden feeling that one must urinate immediately. Young children's urinary control is often not strong enough to counteract this sensation, and the result can be an unexpected rash of accidents. Urinary infections can result in kidney disease if they are not treated promptly. To be on the safe side, call your doctor. Your doctor may ask you to collect a urine sample in a sterile container to be tested so that infection can be ruled out.

Page 107:

You sleep for a long time. Sometimes you wake up and your bed is wet. That's because you made wee-wee while you were sleeping. Call to Mommy and Daddy and one of us will change your pajamas and your sheets so they'll be nice and dry. If you wake up and need to go to the bathroom, call to Daddy and Mommy. One of us will take you there. That way you can be nice and dry all night long.

The child should be kept in diapers at night until you begin to find that she's usually dry in the morning. Depending on the child, this may take several months — or several years. Many normal children are not dry all night till age 5, 6, or even later.

In the seventeenth century, French medical authorities warned parents not to beat a little boy "excessively" for wetting their beds, lest a child tie a cord around his penis to prevent accidents. To cure children of bed-wetting, the Delaware Indians fed them pieces of roasted timber rat. Among the Chaga, who live on the slopes of Mount Kilimanjaro in northern Tanzania, today's mother collects raindrops in the hoof of a goat or cow and gives it to the child, explaining that it contains magic that will put an end to wet beds. Any of these approaches is far more sensible than those some parents use to try to control bed-wetting. To see why, it's necessary to understand the way in which children attain night control of the bladder.

For a child to sleep until morning without urinating, the bladder must be large enough to hold all of the urine produced during the night. It has been theorized that part of the increase in bladder capacity which allows a child to be dry at night takes

55

place as the child learns to hold in during the daytime. As more urine flows from the kidneys to the bladder, the effect is as if a balloon were connected to a dripping water faucet: the bladder stretches. Over the course of the child's toilet-learning experience the bladder gradually grows and stretches enough to hold a night's production of urine.

The traditional ways of "training" children to remain dry at night include stopping fluids after the late afternoon, "picking up" the child during the night, punishments for wet nights and rewards for dry ones. A noted pediatric urologist has described these as methods which "benefit the bed, not the child."

The problem with these techniques is that instead of helping the child increase bladder capacity, they hinder. Eliminating fluids after the late afternoon — besides being properly classifiable as cruel and unusual punishment, not to mention being awful for the child's kidneys — accomplishes just the opposite of what is desired. Night kidney output is drastically reduced, thus giving the child no opportunity to learn to hold in a normal night's output of urine.

The same goes for "picking up" the child. Aside from the fact that few adults would appreciate being dragged out of bed, plunked dazed and blinking on the commode, and commanded to excrete, the method doesn't work. To begin with, there's no button you can push to get a child to urinate on cue. Waiting for a child to go when you are tired and want to sleep has to be far more exasperating than tossing a sheet in the washing machine in the morning. Even if picking the child up does save washing sheets, it will keep the child from developing more bladder capacity through being allowed to sleep soundly while a full night's quota of urine drips into the bladder. It's far more logical to encourage the child to urinate just before bedtime, so that the night begins with an empty bladder. Punishing or rewarding a child in the morning for her behavior while unconscious confuses the child and makes the parent seem inconsistent in the child's eyes.

The counterproductiveness of benefiting the bed rather than the child is underlined by the interesting theory that the wet bed itself helps in achieving night control. The sensation of lying in wet pajamas is unpleasant — in psychological terminology, "aversive." Every time the child has this experience, she unconsciously learns to avoid it by holding in her urine. The feeling of wetness, or irritation caused by the urine, may then wake some children, in which case another aversive stimulus comes into play: the annoyance of being awakened from a good sleep. The child thus gradually learns to control her bladder in order to avoid having her sleep disturbed. In other words, allowing the child to wet the bed may, ironically, itself be an important method of teaching night control: by wetting the bed, the child learns not to wet the bed.

It shouldn't be surprising that several carefully conducted medical studies have shown that there is little or no relationship between parental "training" efforts and the normal development of night control. Keep in mind that a large number of children sleep for so many hours that even as their bladder capacity increases normally, it is still not large enough to contain the urine produced during the abnormally long nights. The only thing that will "cure" them of bed-wetting is the reduction of the length of sleep that takes place naturally as they grow older. As a mother in Zaïre told a psychologist who had "searched in vain for a single exhortation to the child to stay dry at night": "That will come little by little by itself."

A prescription drug called imipramine hydrochloride has been used in an attempt to control bed-wetting. This drug, commonly known by the trade name Tofranil, acts on the child's central nervous system to produce urinary retention artificially. Imipramine can be an extremely dangerous substance. There have been a number of fatal and near-fatal accidental poisonings of children who were being treated with it. One medical journal article was titled, "Poisoning as a Complication of Enuresis." Nearly all of the victims reported have been 2½ years old — an age at which bed-wetting is perfectly normal, far too early for treatment with powerful drugs to have been medically advisable, if indeed it is ever desirable. Imipramine in large doses has a particularly poisonous effect on the heart, and children who have survived the first effects of this "complication" of bed-wetting have had to remain in intensive care for up to four days.

The most effective way to work for night control is to concentrate on day control. To help your child's bladder expand enough for her to stay dry all night, make sure she drinks plenty of liquids during the daytime, and that she isn't encouraged to urinate so often that she seldom has a chance to "hold it in." Parents who put their kids on the pot frequently, demanding that they empty their bladders, may, unknowingly, be setting the stage for bed-wetting problems later on.

One factor to keep in mind as you guide your child in toilet learning is that stress and anxiety during the child's early years — particularly between the second and third birthdays — have often been associated with prolonged bed-wetting. Stressful situations — illness or injury, separation from a parent, the arrival of a new sister or brother, moving to a new home —can set up anxieties which may interfere with the delicate learning process that eventually results in night control. If one or more such events occurs before or during toilet learning, be particularly sensitive to your child's emotional state. More encouragement, soothing words and hugs, and less pressure of all kinds, particularly in the area of toilet learning will make future bed-wetting less likely.

When your child does wet the bed, which is inevitable in the first stages of toilet learning, just change the sheets and forget it happened. And as in every other area of toilet learning, whatever you do, don't tongue-lash, ridicule, or punish your child for something she couldn't help. After all — she was sound asleep.

Page 108:
In the morning, first thing, go to the bathroom. Just like Mommy and Daddy.

When you get to the stage when the child no longer wears a diaper at night, make sure she gets to the bathroom as soon as she wakes up. No sense holding it in all night just to have an accident in the morning. Many parents hear that their child has woken up, but roll over and try to catch a few more winks. The way to get the most rest in the long run, however, is to drag yourself out of bed and make sure you get your child to the bathroom before she loses control and the feeling of accomplishment she'll gain by getting to the toilet in time.

It has often been suggested that children are supposed to have a bowel movement every morning. Don't be concerned if your child doesn't move her bowels at the same time every day. Some kids move them several times a day, usually at different times. Even if the child skips a day, it's nothing to be alarmed about. Some children, in fact, go only every other day or two.

Page 109:
You've been doing very well. Soon you'll be dry all the time. Won't that be nice? "I'm happy!" says the little girl. "I don't have to wear a diaper any more."

The printed text reads, "says the little girl." Depending on the sex of your child, you can say, "says the little boy."

As your child becomes skilled at each new step in toilet learning, you praise her and let her know that you're pleased. But gradually you'll phase out expressions of approval for going to the bathroom. The time to praise your child will be when she stays dry between changes of clothing. The idea isn't for the child to be running to the toilet all the time, but to be dry all the time.

❀

Finish your presentation of Part 2 by making a big point of giving this book to your child as a present. You can say, "Now we're going to give you this book for your very own. You can read it as much as you want — because it's all about you." Though kids of toilet learning age can't read yet, they can "read" pictures surprisingly well. When you go over Part 2 together again, as you should do often during toilet learning, your child will undoubtedly have her own stories to tell you about what's going on in each picture. Listen carefully to the way she interprets the pictures and you will get a sense of the progress your child is making in absorbing the information contained in Part 2.

Finally, when people ask, "Is your child toilet trained?" you can say, "No — but she has learned how to use the toilet."

If you would like to share your experiences in toilet learning, please write to the following address:

Alison Mack
TOILET LEARNING
121 Eileen Way
Syosset, NY 11791

2

Child's Guide to Toilet Learning

Look — the little girl is playing.
She's having fun.

She feels nice and dry in her diaper.

Uh-oh! The little girl just went in her diaper!
She feels wet and sticky.
She doesn't look happy, does she?

Being wet and sticky in your diaper doesn't feel good, does it?
You like to feel nice and dry.

We will show you what to do so you can feel nice and dry.
Let's sit down and learn from this book.

What's in your diaper comes out of you.

Part of the food you eat comes out of you.
Look — people eating.

The food you eat is made into

Bones to make you big

Teeth to chew with

Hair to comb

Nails to cut

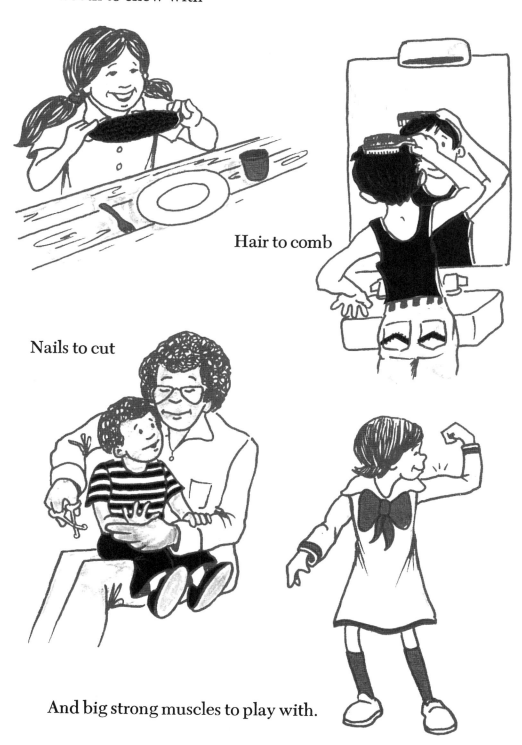

And big strong muscles to play with.

Anything you don't need goes out of you.
(See the wee-wee coming out of the dog?)

One of the things that comes out of you is wet.
We call it wee-wee.

See the rain puddle?
Rain is wet.

The other thing that comes out of you is sticky.
We call it doo-doo.
(See the horse making doo-doo?)

When wee-wee and doo-doo are in your diaper,
they make you feel wet and sticky.
You don't like it.
You want to feel nice and dry.
When you were little, if you were wet and sticky,
you had to call for Mommy and Daddy to help you.

You wore diapers.

We had to change you,

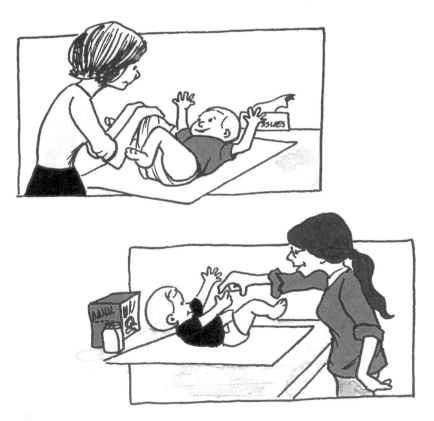

so you could feel nice and dry.

Soon you're going to wear underpants.

Just like Mommy.

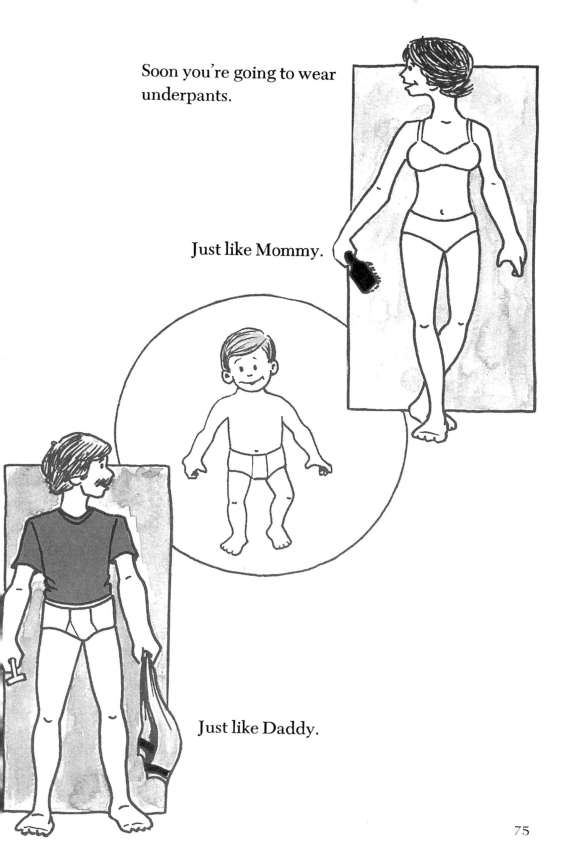

Just like Daddy.

When you feel like you've got to make wee-wee or doo-doo, you will help yourself by going to the bathroom.

In the bathroom there's a toilet.
The toilet is there so nobody in our home has to be wet and sticky.
We put our wee-wee and doo-doo in the toilet.

The toilet is round.
It has water in it.

It has a seat that goes up and down.
It has a cover.

Before you use the toilet
you pull your pants down
all the way.

Little girls sit on the toilet
when they make wee-wee and doo-doo . .

Just like Mommy.

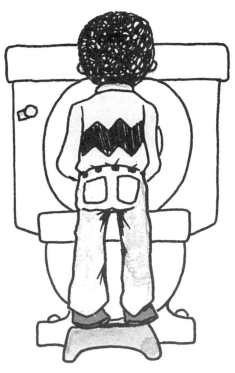

Little boys stand in front of the toilet when they make wee-wee

and sit when they make doo-doo . . .

Just like Daddy.

Brian makes wee-wee and doo-doo in a potty
which is like a little toilet.

After you go,
you take toilet paper and wipe yourself
so you'll be nice and clean.
Then you drop the paper in the toilet.

When you're all done,
you get off the toilet and pull your pants up.
Then you pull the handle on the toilet
and make it go "*Whoosh!*"

84 In the city, the wee-wee and doo-doo go out of the toilet

into a big pipe, underneath the ground.

In the country the wee-wee and doo-doo go
out of the toilet
right into the ground.

Everybody goes to the bathroom.

Firemen go to the bathroom.

Policemen go to the bathroom.

Babysitters go to the bathroom.

People on TV go to the bathroom.

The mailman goes to the bathroom.

Grandpa goes to the bathroom.

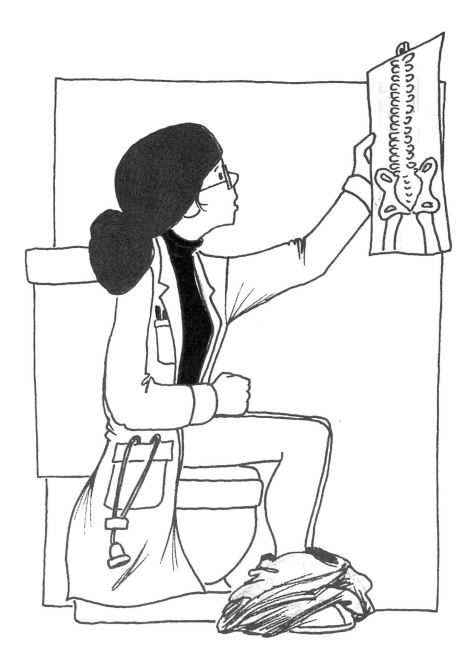

Doctors go to the bathroom.

Grandma goes to the bathroom.

After they are all done on the toilet,
they wash their hands
so they'll be nice and clean.

Just like you.

Almost everywhere you go there are bathrooms.

In a restaurant . .

In a gas station there are bathrooms.

There's a bathroom in a plane . . .
In a big boat . . .
In a train . . .
In a big bus . . .

There are bathrooms at the zoo.

WOMEN

MEN

Sometimes when you're outside,
you've got to make wee-wee or doo-doo.

If there's no bathroom,
you can make wee-wee and doo-doo on the ground,
like all the animals do.
Look — the deer is making wee-wee in the woods.

From now on,
when you feel like you want to make wee-wee or doo-doo,
don't go in your underpants.
Hold it in as hard as you can,
and come to Daddy and Mommy.
Say, "I want to go to the bathroom."
We will take you there.

"Daddy," the little boy says, "Sometimes I
can't hold it in till I get to the bathroom."

"That's okay," says the Daddy.
"If you go in your underpants, don't worry.
Just tell us so we can give you nice dry clothes.
Soon you'll be able to hold it in better and better."

You sleep for a long time.
Sometimes you wake up and your bed is wet.
That's because you made wee-wee while you were sleeping.
Call to Mommy and Daddy
and one of us will change your pajamas and your sheets
so they'll be nice and dry.

If you wake up and need to go to the bathroom,
call to Daddy and Mommy.
One of us will take you there.
That way you can be nice and dry all night long.

In the morning, first thing,
go to the bathroom.
Just like Mommy and Daddy.